Olympiad Planner

10

for
(MATHEMATICS, SCIENCE, CYBER, AND ENGLISH OLYMPIADS)

Editorial Board

V&S PUBLISHERS

Published by:

V&S PUBLISHERS

F-2/16, Ansari road, Daryaganj, New Delhi-110002
☎ 23240026, 23240027 • *Fax:* 011-23240028
Email: info@vspublishers.com • *Website:* www.vspublishers.com

Regional Office : Hyderabad
5-1-707/1, Brij Bhawan (Beside Central Bank of India Lane)
Bank Street, Koti, Hyderabad - 500 095
☎ 040-24737290
E-mail: vspublishershyd@gmail.com

Branch Office : Mumbai
Jaywant Industrial Estate, 2nd Floor–222, Tardeo Road
Opposite Sobo Central Mall, Mumbai – 400 034
☎ 022-23510736
E-mail: vspublishersmum@gmail.com

Follow us on:

All books available at **www.vspublishers.com**

ISBN 978-93-579409-7-9

Printed at : Param Offseters Okhla New Delhi-110020

Publisher's Note

V&S Publishers, after the grand success of a number of Academic and General books, is pleased to bring out Olympiad Planners for classes from 1st to 10th under The Gen X series – generating Xcellence in generation X – which helps students to prepare for the Olympiad exams. The planner provides step-wise guidance to go through the exam i.e. *how to register, tips and study chart for efficient preparation, pattern and syllabus of exam, recommended study material and scholarships*. One model paper on Mathematics, Science, Cyber and English Olympiad each has been included for practice purpose.

All planners have been developed to provide systematic guidance to the students who aspire to become Olympiad champs at national and international levels. To get success in Olympiads, students need to do thorough study of topics covered in Olympiad syllabus and the topics covered in school syllabus as well. The tips and tricks given in this planner help candidates to prepare for the exam efficiently. Olympiads check efficiency of candidates in problem solving. These exams are conducted in different stages at regional, national, and international levels. At each stage of the exam, a candidate should be fully prepared to take new challenges. Thus, this exam requires careful attention towards comprehension of concepts and thorough practice.

We wish you all success in the examination and a very bright future.

All the best

Contents

1 Introduction to Olympiad 7
2. How to Apply 10
3. Selection Procedure 13
4. Syllabus and Curriculum 16
5. Pattern of Exam 18
6. Study Chart for Efficient Preparation 21
7. Tips to Crack Olympiads 27
8. Study Material for Olympiads 30
9. Awards and Scholarships 32
10. Model Test Paper (IMO) 36
11. Model Test Paper (NSO) 41
12. Model Test Paper (NCO) 50
13. Model Test Paper (IEO) 55

1 Introduction to Olympiads

International Mathematical Olympiad (IMO)

International Mathematical Olympiad (IMO) is a world championship mathematics competition for students of High School and it is held annually in different countries. The first IMO with seven participating countries was held in 1959 in Romania. The scope of this exam was gradually expanded to over 100 countries within five continents. The IMO Advisory Board ensures that the competition takes place every year and that each host country observes regulations and traditions of the IMO.

In India, Mathematics Olympiad is conducted by **Homi Bhabha Centre for Science Education (HBCSE)** which organises this exam on behalf of **National Board for Higher Mathematics (NBHM)** of the Department of Atomic Energy (DAE). **Central Board of Secondary Education (CBSE)** also conducts Group Mathematical Olympiad based on which successful candidates are sent to the International Mathematical Olympiad. A maximum of 30 students from CBSE group are selected (strictly in order of merit) to participate in Indian National Mathematical Olympiad (INMO) conducted by National Board of Higher Mathematics (NBHM). The selection at national level leads to participation at International Mathematical Olympiad. **Science Olympiad Foundation (SOF)** which identifies and encourages mathematical creativity of children also conducts Mathematics Olympiad in schools across India and abroad.

The students from classes 1–12 are eligible to appear in Maths Olympiad. For classes 1–4, 10 questions from Section–1 (Logical Reasoning), 10 questions from Section–2 (Mathematical Reasoning), 10 questions from Section–3 (Everyday Mathematics) and 5 questions from Section–4 (Achievers section) are asked. Thus, the students are required to answer 35 questions in 60 minutes.

For classes 5–12, 15 questions from Section–1 (Logical Reasoning), 20 questions from Section–2 (Mathematical Reasoning), 10 questions from Section–3 (Everyday Mathematics) and 5 questions from Section–4 (Achievers section) are asked. Thus, the students are required to answer 50 questions in 60 minutes.

National Science Olympiad (NSO)

The National Science Olympiad (NSO) is a science competition in Asia. It is conducted in two levels. The students from classes 1–12 are eligible to appear in it. For classes 1– 4, 5 questions from Section–1 (Logical Reasoning) and 25 questions from Section–2 (Science) and 5 questions from Section–3 (Achievers section) are asked in the exam. Thus, the students are required to answer 35 questions in 60 minutes. For classes 5–10, 10 questions from Section–1 (Logical Reasoning) and 35 questions from Section–2 (Science) and 5 questions from Section–3 (Achievers section) are asked. Thus, the students are required to answer 50 questions in 60 minutes. The questions are of Multiple Choice Questions (MCQs) type and students are required to mark their responses on OMR answer sheets.

All the students participating in NSO (1st level) get a Student Performance Report (SPR), with their Score, School Rank, City Rank, State Rank, International Rank and Percentile, as well as a Certificate of Participation. SOF also generates a performance report for all participating schools, known as School Performance Report (SCPR). On the basis of 1st level exam, Gold, Silver and Bronze medals are awarded to 1st, 2nd and 3rd rank holder (with minimum 10 enrolments in the concerned class) and Gold medal to every class topper (if 5–9 students have enrolled) in each participating school. Selected students appear for 2nd level examination and according to 2nd level ranks, the prizes are given. The criteria for selection to 2nd level are as follows: the student should have secured International Rank from 1–500 (both inclusive) and/or State Rank from 1–10 (both inclusive) and/or Student should secure 1st, 2nd or 3rd rank (minimum ten enrollments) and/ or a minimum of 30% of total marks. All students participating in NSO (2nd level) are also given a Certificate of Merit. The respective school of each student with International Rank from 1–3 (both inclusive) is awarded a Science Intellect Trophy (SIT) for having the winning students on their rolls.

Thus, Olympiad is a platform that identifies young geniuses and provides them with a unique competitive platform where they can prove themselves.

National Cyber Olympiad (NCO)

National Cyber Olympiad (NCO) is an international championship competition that identifies Cyber Savvy talents. The NCO is an academic and scholastic aptitude competition which is held to identify extraordinary skills of students and to provide them a distinction. This exam is conducted to search talented students in computer education and to encourage them to develop their careers in this field. The students from classes 2–12 are eligible to appear in it. It is conducted in two levels. At the 1st level of exam, for classes 2–4, 5 questions from Section–1 (Logical Reasoning), 25 questions from Section–2 (Computer and IT) and 25 questions from Section–3 (Achievers section) are asked whereas for classes 5–12, 10 questions from Section–1 (Logical Reasoning), 35 questions from Section–2 (Computer and IT), 5 questions from Section–3 (Achievers section) are asked. The students are required to answer a total of 50 questions in 60 minutes and there is no negative marking for incorrect answers. Questions are of Multiple Choice Questions (MCQs) type and students are required to mark their responses on OMR answer sheets.

In India, NCO is conducted by Science Olympiad Foundation (SOF) which identifies and encourages children to enhance their skills in Cyber and IT. This exam assesses a student at national level. The national level assessment gives students a fair idea of the position where he/she stands in comparison to other students and inspires him/her to score better marks.

International English Olympiad (IEO)

International English Olympiad (IEO) is an examination of the first of its kind in the history of English language testing in India. The IEO is a joint venture of the Science Olympiad Foundation and The English and Foreign Languages University (EFLU), Hyderabad. The examination has been developed by a group of professionals who constitute the All India English Language Testing Authority (AIELTA) at The English and Foreign Languages University (EFLU).

The students from classes 1–12 are eligible to appear in International English Olympiad. For classes 1–4, 30 MCQs from Sections 1–3 (Word and Structure Knowledge, Reading, Spoken and Written Expression) and 5 MCQs from Section–4 (Achievers section) are asked whereas for classes 5–12, 45 MCQs are asked from Sections 1–3 (Word and Structure Knowledge, Reading and Spoken and Written Expression) and 5 MCQs from Section–4 (Achievers section) are asked.

2 How to Apply

Registration: The IMO is open to students from 1st to 12th standard. The prospectus containing the registration forms is sent to all the schools which are registered with SOF. The schools which are not registered may also request for prospectus by sending an e-mail at *info@sofworld.org* or by making a phone call to SOF.

Registration of New Schools: The schools which want to participate in the Olympiad are required to send their complete address in the following format.

- School Name : ______________
- Address : ______________
- City : ______________
- State : ______________
- Pin code : ______________
- Phone No. with STD Code : ______________
- E-mail : ______________
- Principal's Name : ______________

The SOF will send relevant information and registration forms to the school at appropriate time. The registration forms duly filled in and complete in all respects must be submitted to the SOF by the due date. Last date of receipt of registrations is 30 days before the chosen date of exam.

Roll Numbers: The school's coordinator (teacher) generates students' Roll Numbers as per the guidelines. A copy of these roll numbers along with the Students' Registration Sheet (SRS) and School Registration Form (SRF) should be sent to the Foundation's office on/before the due date of submission of forms. The Foundation will register the applicant school and the students and will dispatch question papers and guidelines for conducting the examination.

Note: Principals/teachers of all participating schools may please note that any school can be registered as a centre for IMO. No fee is required from the institution to be a registered examination centre. For a school to become the centre, at least 10 students need to be registered from the school for feasibility reasons. The IMO is conducted in two days for Level 1. Every school may select a date for conducting the IMO exam as per its convenience. A different question paper will be provided to the students on each day.

The students should register through their respective schools only. An individual registration by students is not acceptable.

Fee Structure

For schools in India: A nominal fee is charged from each student. The school shall retain a part of it per student per Olympiad for its expenses as exam centre. The details about fee/mode of payment etc. are given in detail in Registration Forms sent to the schools.

Mode of Payment: The school can make payment via Demand Draft or through NEFT/ RTGS

- **Demand Draft:** It should be made in favour of **Science Olympiad Foundation** payable at **New Delhi.**
- **NEFT/ RTGS:** Details for NEFT/RTGS are:
  - Beneficiary Name : Science Olympiad Foundation
  - Beneficiary A/C No. : SOFXXXXXX (XXXXXX denotes school Code allotted by Science Olympiad Foundation)
  - Beneficiary Bank Name : ICICI Bank
  - Beneficiary Branch : CMS
  - IFSC Code : ICIC0000103

Schedule of Examination

The schools may select a date for conducting the Olympiads in their school premises. The change in date is not permitted. There are separate question papers for different dates. The participating schools may send registrations latest by 31st August every year.

For knowing the date and schedule of exam, students are advised to contact the co-ordinator of their school.

OR

Visit www.sofworld.org for updates on dates, schedule, and pattern of exam etc.

The schedule of Olympiad exams for 2015-16 is as follows:

1st Level Exams:

EXAM NAME	DATE 1	DATE 2
15th NCO	23rd Sept 2015	8th Oct 2015
18th NSO	20th Oct 2015	5th Nov 2015
9th IMO	26th Nov 2015	10th Dec 2015
6th IEO	20th Jan 2016	28th Jan 2016

2nd Level Exams:

2nd level exam was held on 2nd/ 3rd Sunday of Feb 2016. The 2nd level exam is held for students from classes 3rd to 12th for NCO, NSO and IMO. IEO is a single level exam.

3 Selection Procedure

Selection Procedure for IMO

The selection of student would be done on the basis of performance in the exam. Results of both levels of IMO are declared within 6 weeks of the examination.

- The results are sent to the concerned schools.
- The results are also made available on SOF's website.

International Mathematics Olympiad is conducted in 2 Levels/phases.

Level 1: The first level of the test is organized in the respective schools of the participants during school hours.

(i) The level 1 competition is a written objective type test of 60 minutes' duration comprising 35 objective-type (Multiple Choice) questions for class 2 to class 4 and 50 objective-type (Multiple Choice) questions for class 5 to class 12.

(ii) The question paper consists of:

(a) Logical Reasoning (b) Mathematical Reasoning (c) Everyday Mathematics (d) Achievers Section

(iii) There are separate question papers for each class.

(iv) The medium of the test is English.

(v) CBSE, ICSE/ISC and State Board syllabus is followed for setting the test papers.

(vi) The exam is conducted during school hours.

Level 2: The qualifiers to second round include the following:

(i) Top 5% of candidates class-wise, who appear for the 1st level exam. Due weight-age to marks scored in different sections will be given. Each section is accorded with separate weight-age.

(ii) State-wise top 10 rank holders class-wise.

(iii) Class topper where at least 10 students from a class appear in the exam and scores 75% qualifying marks.

Selection Procedure For NSO

Level 1: The first level of the test is organized in respective schools of participants during school hours.

(i) The level 1 competition is a written objective type test of 60 minutes duration comprising 35 objective type (Multiple Choice) questions for class 2 to class 4 and 50 objective type (Multiple Choice) questions for class 5 to class 12.

(ii) The question paper for class 1st to class 10th consists of:

(a) Logical Reasoning (b) Science (c) Achievers section

(iii) There are separate question papers for each class.

(iv) The medium of the test is English.

(v) CBSE, ICSE/ISC and State Board syllabus is followed for setting test papers.

(vi) The exam is conducted during school hours.

Level 2: The qualifiers to second round would include the following:

(i) Top 5% of candidates class-wise, who appear for the 1st level exam. Due weight-age to marks scored in different sections will be given. Each section is accorded with separate weight-age.

(ii) State-wise top 10 rank holders class-wise.

(iii) Class topper where at least 10 students from a class appear in the exam scores 75% qualifying marks.

Selection Procedure for NCO

National Cyber Olympiad is conducted in 2 Levels

Level 1: The first level of the test is organized in respective schools of participants during school hours.

(i) The level 1 competition is a written objective type test of 60 minutes duration comprising 35 objective type (Multiple Choice) questions for class 2 to class 4 and 50 objective type (Multiple Choice) questions for class 5 to class 12.

(ii) The question paper consists of :

(a) Logical Reasoning
(b) Computer and Information Technology
(c) Achievers Section

(iii) There are separate question papers for each class.

(iv) The medium of the test is English.

(v) CBSE, ICSE/ISC and State Board syllabus is followed for setting the test papers.

(vi) The exam is conducted during school hours.

Level 2: The qualifiers to second round would include the following

(i) Top 5% students who appear for the 1st level exam from every class

(ii) State-wise top 10 performing students from each class

(iii) Topper of each class where at least 10 students have appeared for the exam

Selection Procedure for IEO

Criteria for ranking in 2nd level Olympiad exams:

In case of 2nd level exams, ranks will be accorded on the basis of following criteria:

(i) Total Marks scored in 2nd level exam

In case of a tie of marks, ranks will be finalized as per following order:

(a) Marks scored in sections of 2nd level exam accord more priority.

(b) Total Marks scored in level 1 exam

(c) Marks scored in sections in level 1 exam accord more priority

(d) Past performance of student

(e) Date of Birth - Younger student gets higher priority

Note: In 2nd level, no two students will be given the same rank.

Criteria for ranking- single level Olympiad exams:

For IEO and class 1 and 2 students appearing in NCO, NSO and/or IMO exams, ranks will be accorded on the following criteria:

(i) Marks obtained in the exam.

In case two or more students score same number of marks, ranks will be determined on the following criteria:

(a) Marks obtained in different sections of the exam. Each section is accorded separate priority.

(b) Student's performance in school during previous year - as mentioned in the OMR. This may be verified at the discretion of SOF. Student not stating past year's performance may not be considered for ranking in case of a tie.

(c) Age of student - with greater preference being given to younger student.

(d) Telephonic or personal Interview may be conducted.

No two students will be given same rank. However, in case two or more students score equally on all parameters defined above, the award may be distributed equally among all winners.

4 Syllabus and Curriculum

IMO Class-10

Section 1: Verbal and Non-Verbal Reasoning

Section 2: Mathematical Reasoning: Real Numbers, Polynomials, Pair of Linear Equations in Two Variables, Quadratic Equations, Arithmetic Progressions, Triangles, Coordinate Geometry, Introduction to Trigonometry, Some Applications of Trigonometry, Circles, Constructions, Areas Related to Circles, Surface Areas and Volumes, Statistics, Probability.

Section 3: Everyday Mathematics: The Syllabus of this section will be based on the syllabus of Mathematical Reasoning and Quantitative Aptitude.

Section 4: Achievers Section: Higher Order Thinking Questions - Syllabus as per Section – 2.

NSO Class-10

Section 1: Verbal and Non-Verbal Reasoning

Section2: Science: Chemical Reactions and Equations, Acids, Bases and Salts, Metals and Non-metals, Carbon and its Compounds, Periodic Classification of Elements, Life Processes, Reproduction in Organisms, Heredity and Evolution, Light-Reflection and Refraction, Human Eye and Colourful World, Electricity, Magnetic Effects of Electric Current, Sources of Energy, Our Environment and its Management.

Section 3: Achievers Section: Higher Order Thinking Questions - Syllabus as per Section–2.

NCO Class-10

Section 1: Verbal and Non-Verbal Reasoning

Section 2: Computer and IT: Fundamentals of Computer, Operating System, Word Processing Tool, Networking, MS-PowerPoint, MS-Excel, HTML, Internet, Database Management System(Functions, Types, MS-Access), Latest Developments in the field of IT.

Section 3: Achievers Section: Higher Order Thinking Questions - Syllabus as per Section–2.

Questions are based on Windows 7 and MS-Office 2010.

IEO Class-10

Section 1: Word and Structure Knowledge: Synonyms, Antonyms, Analogies and Spellings, One Word, Word order, Nouns, Verbs, Adverbs, Adjectives, Articles, Prepositions, Conjunctions, Punctuations, Voices, Narration. Concord, Question forms, Tenses, Conditionals, Modals, Collocations, Phrasal verbs, Idioms, Homonyms and homophones, Words related to weather, Countries, Language and people, Global problems, etc.

Section 2: Reading: Search for and retrieve information from various text types like Encyclopedias, Dictionaries, etc., Understand information presented in instruction manual format, Message format and others , Acquire broad understanding of and look for specific information in longer texts like editorials, Essays, etc., Make inferences from advanced texts.

Section 3: Spoken and Written Expression: Ability to understand situation-based variations in functions like Giving/accepting compliments, Agreeing, Disagreeing, Requesting, Seeking information, Pronunciation etc.

Section 4: Achievers Section: Higher Order Thinking Questions - Syllabus as per Sections 1, 2 and 3.

5 Pattern of Exam

International Mathematics Olympiad

SOF LEVEL 1

Class	Section	No. of Questions	Marks Per Question	Total Marks
1 to 4	Logical Reasoning	10	1	10
	Mathematical Reasoning	10	1	10
	Everyday Mathematics	10	1	10
	Achievers Section	5	2	10
	Grand Total	**35**		**40**
5 to 12	Logical Reasoning	15	1	15
	Mathematical Reasoning	20	1	20
	Everyday Mathematics	10	1	10
	Achievers Section	5	3	15
	Grand Total	**50**		**60**

SOF LEVEL 2

Class	Section	No. of Questions	Marks Per Question	Total Marks
3 to 4	Mathematics	30	1	30
	Achievers Section	5	2	10
	Grand Total	**35**		**40**
5 to 12	Mathematics	45	1	45
	Achievers Section	5	3	15
	Grand Total	**50**		**60**

National Science Olympiad

Class	Section	No. of Questions	Marks/ question	Total Marks
1 to 4	Logical Reasoning	5	1	5
	Science	25	1	25
	Achievers Section	5	2	10
	Grand Total	**35**		**40**
5 to 10	Logical Reasoning	10	1	10
	Science	35	1	35
	Achievers Section	5	3	15
	Grand Total	**50**		**60**
11 and 12	Physics & Chemistry	25	1	25
	Achievers Section	5	3	15
	Mathematics/Biology	20	1	20
	Grand Total	**50**		**60**

National Cyber Olympiad

NCO LEVEL 1

Class	Section	No. of Questions	Marks per Question	Total Marks
2 to 4	Logical Reasoning	5	1	5
	Computers & IT	25	1	25
	Achievers Section	5	2	10
	Grand Total	35		40
5 to 12	Logical Reasoning	10	1	10
	Computers & IT	35	1	35
	Achievers Section	5	3	15
	Grand Total	50		60

NCO LEVEL 2

Class	Section	No. of Questions	Marks per Question	Total Marks
3 to 4	Computers & IT	30	1	30
	Achievers Section	5	2	10
	Grand Total	**35**		**40**
5 to 12	Computers & IT	45	1	45
	Achievers Section	5	3	15
	Grand Total	**50**		**60**

International English Olympiad

Class	Section	No. of Questions	Marks per Question	Total Marks
1 to 4	Word and Structure Knowledge	30	1	30
	Reading			
	Spoken and Written Expression			
	Achievers Section	5	2	10
	Grand Total	**35**		**40**
5 to 12	Word and Structure Knowledge	45	1	45
	Reading			
	Spoken and Written Expression			
	Achievers Section	5	3	15
	Grand Total	**50**		**60**

6 Study Chart for Efficient Preparation

IMO CLASS–10

	Week 1 	Week 2 	Week 3 	Week 4 	Week 6 
Day/Time	**Two Hours**	**Two Hours**	**Two Hours**	**Two Hours**	**Two Hours**
Monday	Real Numbers	Quadratic Equation	Co-ordinate Geometry	Surface Area and Volume	Model Test Paper–1
Tuesday	Analogy	Number, Ranking and Time Sequence	Blood Relation	Paper Cutting	Subjective Questions
Wednesday	Polynomials	Arithmetic Progression	Trigonometry	Statistics	Solved Paper–1
Thursday	Classification	Direction Sense Test	Mathematic Operations	Mirror Images	Model Test Paper–1
Friday	Linear Equation in Two Variables	Triangles	Circle	Probability	Solved Paper–1
Saturday	Coding, Decoding	Alphabet Test	Series	Achievers Section	
Sunday	Revision	Revision	Revision	Revision	

Note:

- Students can apply this Study Chart for efficient preparation of Olympiad with their regular studies. This chart has been developed by experienced teachers. The choice of topics may vary from one individual to another.
- The students must follow the above study plan and revise it accordingly, for perfection in the subject and they must take balanced diet during their exams.

How to Study

The students, aspiring for IMO should keep the following points in mind, during their preparation:

1. Follow the study plan given to you. For IMO exam, a sincere study of 2 to 2.5 hours daily is sufficient.
2. Students must keep care of their course and apart from this, they have to manage time for IMO exam preparation.

Time Management Schedule :

Wake up : 9:30 A.M. (1 hour study)

Before going to bed : 8:30 PM to 10 PM (1:30 hours study)

Go to bed : 10 PM

3. You must take balanced diet during exams and take special care of your health.
4. Do not panic at any stage of your preparation. Believe in yourself.

   With best wishes.................

NSO CLASS–10

	**Week 1** 	**Week 2** 	**Week 3** 	**Week 4** 	**Week 5** 	**Week 6** 
Day/Time	**Three Hours**	**Three Hours**	**Three Hours**	**Three Hours**	**Three Hours**	**Three Hours**
Monday	Light	Magnetic Effects of Electric Current	Acids, Bases and Salts	Periodic Classification of Elements	Heredity and Evolution	Subject-based Question and HOTS Revision
Tuesday	Human Eye and Colourful World	Sources of Energy	Metals and Non-Metals	Life Processes	Our Environment	Achievers Section Revision
Wednesday	Analogy	Coding and Decoding	Direction Sense Test	Blood Relation Test	Series	Revision: Non-verbal Ability
Thursday	Revision of Theory	Revision of Theory	Revision of Theory	Revision of Theory	Revision of Theory	Revision: Verbal Ability
Friday	Classification	Number, Ranking, and Time Sequence Test	Alphabet Test	Mathematical Operations	Paper Folding Paper Cutting	Model Test Paper–1
Saturday	Electricity	Chemical Reactions and Equations	Carbon and Its Compounds	Reproduction in Organisms	Mirror Images	Model Test Paper–2
Sunday	Revision (Duration: 3:00 hrs.)	Revision (Duration: 3:00 hrs.)	Revision (Duration: 3:00 hrs.)	Revision (Duration: 3:00 hrs.)	Subjective revision	Previous year NSO Paper

NCO CLASS–10

	Week 1 	Week 2 	Week 3 	Week 4 
Day/Time	**Two Hours**	**Two Hours**	**Two Hours**	**Three Hours**
Monday	Basic of Information Technology	HTML	Blood Relation	Mirror Images & Water Images
Tuesday	SECTION 1: Unit-2 Introduction to Computers	SECTION 1: Unit-8 MS Access	SECTION 2: Unit-5 Direction Sense Test	Section 2: Unit-12 Non-verbal Test
Wednesday	Input & Output devices	Networking and Multimedia	Analogy	High Order Thinking Skills Short Answer Questions
Thursday	Word Processing Tool	Internet	Classification	National Cyber Olympiad – 2012
Friday	MS PowerPoint	Series Completion	Calendar	National Cyber Olympiad – 2013
Saturday	MS Excel	Coding Decoding	Cubes and Dice	Model Test Paper–1
Sunday	Revision	Alphabet Test and Number Ranking	Figure Pattern	Model Test Paper–2

Note:

- *Identify your weak areas from detailed reports and strengthen the areas.
- *Practice question from huge question bank:
  - (i) MTG Workbooks for Class 10
  - (ii) 'SOF Olympiad Trainer' Mobile Apps
  - (iii) OSDS (Olympiad Skill Development System)
  - (iv) Olympiads' Books of Reasoning (for preparation of the reasoning section of Olympiads)
  - (v) E-Quiz
- *Take more mock tests to improve your efficiency and become fully prepared for the exam.

IEO CLASS – 10

	Week 1	Week 2	Week 3	Week 4	Week 5	Week 6
Day/Time	**Two Hours**	**Two Hours**	**Three Hours**	**Three Hours**	**Three Hours**	**Three Hours**
Monday	Noun	Conjunctions	Voice	Collocations	Vocabulary	Requesting and Seeking Information
Tuesday	Adjective	Phrasal Verbs	Narration	Word Order	Encyclopaedia Dictionary	Pronunciation
Wednesday	Articles	Punctuations	Spellings	Synonyms and Antonyms	Instruction Manual Format, Message Format	High Order Thinking Skills (HOTS)
Thursday	Verb	Tenses	Analogy	Homonyms and Homophones	Editorials Essays Inference from Advanced Texts	Model Test Paper (Time: As per exam Pattern)
Friday	Adverb	Conditionals	Concord	One Word	Giving and Accepting Complements	Solved Paper (Time: As per exam Pattern)
Saturday	Preposition	Modals	Question Forms	Idioms	Agreeing and Disagreeing	Revision
Sunday	Revision	Revision	Revision	Revision	Revision	Revision

7 Tips to Crack Olympiads

Tips to Crack Maths Olympiad

1. Focus on learning the concepts well and on acquiring the basic skills needed to solve problems.
2. Practise mathematics regularly. Make sure that you are solving as many different types of problems as possible. You can practise lots of questions on different topics from the Internet.
3. Identify the areas of your strength and weakness and focus on weak areas to get better results.
4. Solve model papers and understand the pattern of previous years' papers. This will help you to get acquainted with the pattern and structure of the test.
5. Learn shortcuts to solve various types of questions. Keep these points on your fingertips to save time and work efficiently.
6. Read questions thoroughly. Olympiad problems are known for their complexity, which means you have to take an extra effort.
7. During exam do not waste time in solving difficult questions; rather try some short and easy questions first.
8. Do a lot of practice covering each topic. After that take mock tests, analyse your result, and make an assessment report for your current score.
9. Prepare your notes and important facts to remember and do quick revision before exams. It helps in learning faster.

Tips to Crack Science Olympiad

1. Go through the concepts and ponder about them in a practical way.
2. Learn all the formulae and equations well and prepare notes for quick revision.
3. Do experiments in labs to practice and to learn the concepts well.
4. Learn and remember important shortcuts. They should be on your fingertips. It helps you save time and write answers efficiently.

5. Solve Previous Years Papers and Model Test Papers to understand the pattern and structure of the test.
6. Identify your weak areas and try to focus on the topics to overcome the difficulties.
7. Read every question well before answering. Some problems are typical in nature.
8. Do not waste your time in solving difficult questions. First take up easy questions and solve them.
9. Do quick revision before exams. It also helps in learning faster.

Tips to Crack Cyber Olympiad

1. Focus on learning the concepts well and on acquiring the basic skills needed to solve problems.
2. Make sure that you are doing as many different types of problems as possible.
3. Identify the areas of your strength and weakness and focus on weak areas to get better results.
4. Solve model papers and understand the pattern of previous years' papers. This will help you to get acquainted with the pattern and structure of the test.
5. Learn shortcuts to solve various types of questions. Keep these points on your fingertips to save time and work efficiently.
6. Read questions thoroughly. Olympiad problems are known for their complexity, which means you have to take an extra effort.
7. Do not waste time in solving difficult questions; rather try some short and easy questions first.
8. Do a lot of practice covering each topic. After that take mock tests, analyse your results, and make an assessment report for your current score.
9. Practise a lot of questions on different topics in the Olympiad syllabus from the Internet.
10. Prepare your notes and important facts to remember and do quick revision before exams. It helps in learning faster as well.

Tips to Crack English Olympiad

1. Read a newspaper every day. It will help you in understanding different types of sentence structures and will enhance your knowledge as well.
2. Go through one page of dictionary daily to enrich your vocabulary. This will add a lot of new words and their meanings in different contexts to your vocabulary.

3. Speak in English with your friends, parents and teachers. It will help you in learning verbal speaking skills.
4. Read grammar books and novels to learn language skills and grasp diverse contexts and themes.
5. Do a lot of practice on verbal and written English exercises daily.
6. Identify the areas of your strength and weakness and focus on weak areas to get better results.
7. Solve model papers and understand the pattern of previous years' papers. This will help you to get acquainted with the pattern and structure of the test.
8. Learn shortcuts to solve various types of questions. Keep these points on your fingertips to save time and work efficiently.
9. Read questions thoroughly. Olympiad problems are known for their complexity, which means you have to take an extra effort.
10. Do not waste time in solving difficult questions; rather try some short and easy questions first.
11. Prepare your notes and important facts to remember and to do quick revision before exams.

General Tips to Crack Olympiad

1. Go through the syllabus before you start preparation for the exam. For SOF Olympiad, you can visit the www.sofworld.org
2. Start preparations at least two months before the due schedule of the exam; go through all the curriculum books and study material.
3. Go through different books; solve questions that are a little tougher than traditional CBSE type questions.
4. Manage time properly. Time management skills can help you go through the exam successfully.
5. Consult your teachers. Approach your teachers and discuss your issues with him/her. He/she would certainly guide you.
6. Don't stress yourself. Take deep breaths, or eat your favourite ice-cream or even go for a long walk with your friend. Do anything that helps you relax before your exams. It is very important to keep your mind calm before any exam.
7. Read a little more text matter than that of your textbooks in order to gain better insight.
8. Just review everything in brief one day before beginning of the Olympiad test.

8 Study Material for Olympiads

Study Material and Coaching for IMO–10

The following books are recommended for preparation of the Olympiad test:

1. Challenges from the Olympiads by C.R. Pranesachar, S.A. Shirali, B.J. Venkatachala, and C.S. Yogananda
2. Problem Primer for the Olympiad by C.R. Pranesachar, B.J. Venkatachala, and C.S. Yogananda
3. You can also purchase the Olympiad Sample Papers for specific exam from *www.classmantra.com.* You will get the Practice Test and Mock Test.
4. You can purchase a series of books published by V&S Publishers to get precise study material and practice tests on all Olympiads – Mathematics, Science, Cyber, and English.

If any special coaching or tuition is required to become Olympiad Champion?

Though the series of IMO books published by V&S Publishers containing precise concepts with solved examples, illustrations, and diagrams is sufficient for self preparation, the students who find it difficult to learn on their own should go for special coaching/tuition.

Study Material and Coaching for NSO–10

The Olympiad resource books published by V&S Publishers for students of classes 1-10 are very useful for learning the concepts and for doing thorough practice. Each book consists of a lot Multiple Choice Questions based on theory, logical and analytical reasoning.

Salient features of each book:

- *Learning milestones* which enlists the topics covered in the chapter.
- *'Did You Know?'* provides extra information related to the chapter.
- *Test Your Skills and Activities* help children to explore their knowledge base.

- *Concept-based questions* are subjective and enhance the writing and learning skills of a student.
- *HOTS* also known as High Order Thinking Skills questions enrich the out-of-the-box thinking of children.
- Each exercise is divided into two sections:
  (i) MCQs based on the chapter and syllabus
  (ii) MCQS given in the Achievers section deal with extreme logics of the given chapter

If any special coaching or tuition is required to become Olympiad Champion?

Though the series of Science Olympiad books published by V&S Publishers, containing precise concepts with solved examples, illustrations, and diagrams is sufficient for self preparation, the students who find it difficult to learn on their own should go for special coaching/tuition.

Study Material and Coaching for NCO–10

The following books are recommended for Cyber Olympiad:

1. NCO – Olympiad Skill Development System (OSDS) by MTG
2. NCO – Workbooks for practice by MTG
3. BMA's Cyber Olympiad Resource Books

If any special coaching or tuition is required to become Olympiad Champion?

Though the series of Cyber Olympiad books published by V&S Publishers consisting of precise concept with solved examples and explanatory notes for difficult questions is sufficient for self-preparation, yet the students who find it difficult to learn on their own should go for special coaching/tuitions for studying the same.

Study Material and Coaching for IEO–10

If any special coaching or tuition is required to become Olympiad Champion?

Though the series of English Olympiad books published by V&S Publishers containing precise concepts with solved examples and illustrations are sufficient for self preparation, the students who find it difficult to learn on their own should go for special coaching/tuition.

9 Awards and Scholarships

During the academic year 2014-15, over 31500 schools from more than 1400 cities registered and millions of students appeared for the four Olympiad exams. These Olympiads were conducted across 19 countries. For the academic year 2015-16, the SOF will spend over Rupees ten crores on awards, scholarships, gifts and felicitations etc.

All the aspirants participating in IMO (1st level) get a Math Quotient (MQ), their scores and percentile, ranks at city, state, international levels, as well as a certificate of participation. SOF also prepares a performance report known as School Mathematics Quotient for all the participating schools.

The following awards will be provided to the winners of Olympiads being held during the academic year 2015-16.

Awards for Students/IMO Winners

- **For IMO, NSO, and NCO:** International and State toppers (in 20 zones/ states) of classes 3rd to 12th, the awards are given to 2nd level winners.
- **For IEO and winners of IMO, NSO, and NCO class 1st and 2nd:** International and State topper awards will be provided to 1st level winners.
- Each winner will be entitled to one award for an exam. The winners will be entitled to the higher level award only, i.e the international top 3 rank holders will be entitled to awards based on their International ranks. Awards accruing to them for State ranks will be given to the next rank holder. Similarly, school award accruing to a State award winner will be given to the next rank holder.
- All students scoring 100% marks in the 2nd level exams of IMO, NSO, and NCO (1st level exam in IEO) will win special awards consisting of gifts worth Rs.1000/ and Merit Certificates.

Scholarships and Merit Certificates

AT INTERNATIONAL LEVEL		
RANK	**SCHOLARSHIP**	**NO**
1st	Rs.50,000/- each + Gold Medal* + Merit Certificate	47
2nd	Rs.25,000/- each + Silver Medal* + Merit Certificate	47
3rd	Rs.10,000/- each + Bronze Medal* + Merit Certificate	47
AT STATE LEVEL		
RANK	**SCHOLARSHIP**	**NO**
1st	Rs5,000/ - each + Gold Medal* + Merit Certificate	940
2nd	Rs2500/ - each + Silver Medal* + Merit Certificate	940
3rd	Rs1000/ - each + Bronze Medal* + Merit Certificate	940
Rank 4th to 25th	Gifts Worth Rs.1000/- + Merit Certificate	20680

Medals at School Level: 600000 Medals to School Toppers:

- When 10 or more students from one class appear in the exam, *gold, silver and bronze medals are given to top 3 rank holders.
- When 5 to 9 students from a class appear in the exam,* gold medal is given to the top rank holder.

Student Performance Report (SPR)

- Every student who appears in any SOF Olympiad exam is provided with a Student Performance Report (SPR) which is a detailed analysis of how the student attempted in the 1st level Olympiad exam.
- The objective of SPR is to share analysis of performance in the exam with the student and her/his parents. This helps the student knows about the areas of his/her strengths and the areas for improvement on absolute terms and on competitive level consisting of peers from his/her class, who appeared for the Olympiad.

The SPR consists of seven sections:

- **Section A:** This section shows the marks obtained by a student and the rank achieved in school/city/state and at international level.
- **Section B:** This section reveals analysis of a student's performance in the Olympiad exams during past 6 years.

- **Section C**: This section consists of a topic-wise performance score of a student.
- **Section D**: This section provides correct answers to the questions asked in the Olympiad exam, the answers given by the student and performance analysis of student's answers with other students at state and international levels.
- **Section E:** This section provides a percentile score analysis of a student in comparison to class, state and international percentiles.
- **Section F:** This section shows analysis of average marks at school, state and international level.
- **Section G**: This section shows topic-wise performance comparison within a state.

Note:

(i) Participation certificate is given to every student.

(ii) Merit certification is given to 2nd level participants.

(iii) Medals are Gold/Silver/Bronze colour plated as applicable.

(iv) Top 25 rank holders from a class and each Olympiad exam will be awarded Gold Medals of Excellence and Merit Certificates of Excellence. This will be applicable for winners from 20 Zones/States for performance in the 1st level Olympiad in NCO, NSO, IMO and IEO.

Special Scholarships

- **Girl Child Scholarship Scheme (GCSS):** Rs.5000/- scholarship to 300 girls each, who are academically brilliant and come from economically weak families.
- **Scholarship for Excellence in English (SEE):** Rs.5000/- scholarship to 120 students each exhibiting excellence in English Language.
- **SOF Academic Excellence Scholarship (AES):** Rs.5000/ scholarship + Trophy to 160 students from class 3rd to class 10th. The student scoring highest number of marks in 3 Olympiad exams during one year/session wins the AES scholarship. The winners are selected from all 20 zones/ states.

Awards for Schools

At International Level		
Category	**Awards**	**No. of Awards**
Best Principal	Rs.25000/- each + Citation + Trophy	10
Best Teacher	Rs.10000/- each + Citation + Trophy	40
At State Level		
Category	**Awards**	**No. of Awards**
Best Principal	Best Principal Rs.10000/- each + Citation + Trophy	100
Best Teacher	Best Teacher Rs.5000/- each + Citation + Trophy	240
At District Level		
Category	**Awards**	**No. of Awards**
Best Principal	Best Principal Rs.2500/- each + Citation + Trophy	300
Best Teacher	Best Teacher Rs.1000/- each + Citation + Trophy	650

School Performance Report (SPR)

- Every school which appears in any SOF Olympiad exam is provided with a School Performance Report (SPR) which is a detailed analysis of how the students in the school individually and in totality performed in the Olympiad exam.
- The objective of the report is to share analysis of performance of the students with the school authority. This helps the schools assess their strength and focus on the topics in which the students are weak in absolute terms and also on a competitive level vis-à-vis other schools.

The SPR consists of four parts:

1. **Part A:** This shows class-wise/student-wise marks and ranks achieved by students at the city, state and international level.

2. **Part B:** This provides topic-wise average school performance and comparison with other schools with standard deviation at school and international level.
3. **Part C:** This includes an average performance comparison of marks scored by students of a school versus marks scored by other students at the state and at international level.
4. **Part D:** This reveals the depth, section-wise comparison of performance of students of a school and students at state and international levels as well.

Note: Appreciation Mementos to School Principals and Teacher-in-Charge is given also.

10 Model Test Paper (IMO)

1. Choose the correct alternative to fill the missing letters.
_bcc_ac_aabb_ab_cc
(a) *aabca* (b) *abaca*
(c) *bacab* (d) *bcaca*

2. 6, 13, 25, 51, 101 ?
(a) 201 (b) 202
(c) 203 (d) 205

3. Aryabhatta : Mathematician :: Varahamihira : ?
(a) Physician (b) Astronomer
(c) Architect (d) Scientist

4. Choose the correct appropriate description about these three words.
Emu : Gnu : Curlew
(a) These are small insects
(b) These are birds
(c) These are fast runners
(d) These are animal parts

5. In a certain code language BORN is written as APQON and LACK is written as KBBLK. How will the word GRID be written in this code language?
(a) FSHED (b) FSHCD
(c) HSJED (d) FOHCD

6. How many 7*S* are there in the given series which are preceded by 6 which is not preceded by 8?
(a) One (b) Two
(c) Three (d) Four

7. What is the difference between the sum of odd digits and sum of even digits in the number 423578?
(a) 0 (b) 2
(c) 1 (d) 4

8. If ÷ means +, - means +, × means - and + means × then what is the value of
$$\frac{(36\times4)-8\times4}{4+8\times2+16\div1}\ ?$$
(a) 0 (b) 16 (c) 12 (d) 8

9. What is the total number of digits used in numbering the pages of a book having 360 pages?
(a) 1008 (b) 990
(c) 732 (d) 1305

10. Find the missing character.
(a) 9801 (b) 4901
(c) 9901 (d) None of these

11. Which two months in a year have the same calendar?
(a) April, July (b) April, November
(c) June, October (d) April, November

12. How many meaningful words can be formed using the first, third, fifth and sixth letters of the word TRADEMARK using each letter only once in each word?
(a) One (b) Two
(c) Three (d) Four

13. If the alphabet is written in the reverse order and every alternate letter starting with Y is dropped which letter will be exactly in the middle of the remaining letters of the alphabet?
(a) M (b) N
(c) O (d) M or O

14. One morning after sunrise Goyal was standing facing a pole. The shadow of the pole fell exactly to his right. Which direction was he facing?
(a) North (b) South
(c) East (d) West

15. In a certain language, MIRACLE is coded as NKUEHRI then how is GAMBLE coded in that language?

(a) IDOCMF (b) CLEMNK
(c) HCPFQK (d) AELGMN

16. Choose the different numeral pair.
(a) 3152-5321 (b) 7319-9731
(c) 4283-8432 (d) 1975-1579

17. Choose the word which is least like the other words in the group.
(a) Trifle (b) Trilogy
(c) Tricolour (d) Trident

18. Choose the group of the letters which is different from others.
(a) DXCLQZ (b) PFZUBM
(c) NWMBHJ (d) XGKNTY

19. Pointing to a photograph a woman says, "This man's son's sister is my mother-in-law. How is the woman's husband related to the man in the photograph?
(a) Son (b) Grandson
(c) Nephew (d) Son-in-law

20. Rakesh went 15 km to the west from my house, then turned East and walked 25 kms and finally turning left covered 20 kms. How far is he from his house?
(a) 5 km (b) 10 km
(c) 20 km (d) 25 km

21 The value of $\sqrt{6+\sqrt{6+\sqrt{6}}}$ +..... = ?
(a) 4 (b) 3 (c) -2 (d) 5

22. If the 1st, 2nd and last term of an A.P. are a, b and $2a$ respectively. 1st sum is given by
(a) $\frac{3ab}{2(b-a)}$ (b) $\frac{ab}{b-a}$
(c) $\frac{ab}{2(b-a)}$ (d) $\frac{ab}{a+b}$

23. Two circles touch each other externally at C and AB is a common tangent to the circles then $\angle ACB$ = ?
(a) 45° (b) 60°
(c) 30° (d) 90°

24. The angle of elevation of a cloud from a point h metre above a lake is Q. The angle of depression of its reflection in the lake is 45°. The height of the cloud is
(a) $h \tan (45° - q)$ (b) $h \tan (45° + q)$
(c) $h \cot (45° - q)$ (d) $h \cot (45° + q)$

25. From the letters of the word 'MOBILE' a letter is selected. The probability that the letter is a vowel is
(a) $\frac{1}{2}$ (b) $\frac{1}{6}$
(c) $\frac{3}{7}$ (d) $\frac{1}{3}$

26. If points $(a, 0)$, $(0, b)$, and $(1, 1)$ are collinear. then $\frac{1}{a} + \frac{1}{b}$ = ?
(a) 2 (b) 0 (c) 1 (d) -1

27. The curved surface area of a cylinder 264 m^2 and its volume is 924 m^3. The ratio of the diameter to its height is
(a) 3 : 7 (b) 7 : 3
(c) 7 : 6 (d) 6 : 7

28. If mode of a series exceeds it mean by 12 then mode exceeds the median by
(a) 4 (b) 6 (c) 8 (d) 10

29. Mode is
(a) Middle most value
(b) Most frequent value
(c) Least frequent
(d) None of these

30. If $\sin q = \cos q$. What is the value of Q?
(a) 45° (b) 0°
(c) 30° (d) 60°

31. Area of two similar triangles are in the ratio 16:81. What is the ratio of their sides?
(a) 9:4 (b) 4:9
(c) 4:1 (d) 1:4

32. If sin a and cos a are the roots of the eqn $ax^2 + bx + c = 0$ then what is the value of b^2?
(a) $a^2 + 2ac$ (b) a^2-$2ac$
(c) $a^2 + ac$ (d) a^2 - ac

33. If the altitude of the sum is at 60°, then the height of the vertical tower that will cast a shadow of length of 30m is
(a) $30\sqrt{3}$ m (b) 15m
(c) $10\sqrt{3}$ m (d) $15\sqrt{2}$ m

34. If the difference between the radius and circumference of a circle is 37 cm, then its area is

(a) 154 cm^2 (b) 200 cm^2
(c) 150 cm^2 (d) 160 cm^2

35. What is the distance between the points ($a \cos q + b \sin q$, 0) and (0, $a \sin q - b \cos q$)?

(a) $a^2 + b^2$ (b) $a + b$
(c) $a^2 - b^2$ (d) $\sqrt{a^2 + b^2}$

36. The product of the zero of $x^3 + 4x^2 + x - 6$ is

(a) -4 (b) 4
(c) 6 (d) -6

37. If $x + 2$ is a factor of $x^2 + ax + 2b$ and $a + b = 4$, then

(a) $a = 1$ (b) $a = 3, b = 1$
(c) $a = -1, b = 5$ (d) $a = 5, b = -1$

38. The smallest number by which $\sqrt{27}$ should be multiplied so as to get a rational number is

(a) $3\sqrt{3}$ (b) $\sqrt{3}$
(c) $\sqrt{27}$ (d) 3

39. What is the exponent of 2 in the prime factorization of 144?

(a) 4 (b) 5
(c) 6 (d) 3

40. In an equilateral triangle ABC, if $AD \perp BC$, then what is the value of AD^2?

(a) CD^2 (b) $2CD^2$
(c) $3CD^2$ (d) $4CD^2$

41. If $\tan A = \sqrt{2} - 1$ then what is the value of $\sin A \cos A$?

(a) $\frac{1}{2\sqrt{2}}$ (b) $\frac{1}{\sqrt{2}}$
(c) $\frac{1}{2}$ (d) 1

42. What is the mode of the following data
3, 5, 7, 4, 5, 3, 5, 6, 8, 9, 5, 3, 5, 3, 6, 9, 7, 4

(a) 5 (b) 3
(c) 7 (d) 6

43. What is the value of k for which $x^2 + 4x + k$ is a perfect square?

(a) 4 (b) 6
(c) 6 (d) 2

44. What is the sum of n terms of series
$\sqrt{2} + \sqrt{8} + \sqrt{18} + \sqrt{32} + \ldots\ldots$

(a) $\frac{n(n+1)}{2}$ (b) $\frac{n(n+1)}{\sqrt{2}}$
(c) 1 (d) $2n(n+1)$

45. If TP and TQ are two tangents to a circle with centre O so that $\angle POQ = 110°$, then what is the value of $\angle PTQ$?

(a) 80° (b) 90°
(c) 70° (d) 60°

46. The tops of two poles of height 16 m and 10 m are connected by a wire of length l metres if the wire makes an angle of 30° with the horizontal What is the length of wire?

(a) 12 (b) 16
(c) 10 (d) 26

47. A card is accidently dropped from a pack of 52 cards. The probability that it is an ace is

(a) $\frac{1}{4}$ (b) $\frac{1}{52}$
(c) $\frac{12}{13}$ (d) $\frac{1}{13}$

48. If four times the sum of areas of two circular faces of a cylinder of height 8 cm is equal to twice the curved surface area then diameter of the cylinder is

(a) 4 cm (b) 6 cm
(c) 8 cm (d) 2 cm

49. If two zeros of $x^3 + x^2 - 5x - 5$ are $\sqrt{5}$ and $-\sqrt{5}$, then the third root is

(a) 1 (b) 2 (c) -1 (d) 2

50. What is the value of k for which the system of equations $x + 2y = 5$ and $3x + ky + 15 = 0$ has no solution?

(a) -6 (b) 6 (c) 5 (d) $\frac{3}{2}$

Answer Key

1. (c)	2. (c)	3. (a)	4. (b)	5. (a)	6. (c)	7. (c)	8. (a)	9. (b)	10. (a)
11. (a)	12. (d)	13. (b)	14. (b)	15. (c)	16. (d)	17. (a)	18. (b)	19. (b)	20. (b)
21. (b)	22. (a)	23. (d)	24. (b)	25. (a)	26. (c)	27. (b)	28. (c)	29. (b)	30. (a)
31. (b)	32. (b)	33. (a)	34. (a)	35. (d)	36. (c)	37. (b)	38. (b)	39. (a)	40. (c)
41. (a)	42. (a)	43. (a)	44. (b)	45. (c)	46. (a)	47. (d)	48. (c)	49. (c)	50. (b)

11 Model Test Paper (NSO)

Mental Ability Test

1. If in a certain language CARROM is coded as BZQQNL, which word will be coded as HOUSE ?

(a) IRVTE (b) GNTRD
(c) GPTID (d) IPVTF

2. Insert the missing letter

B	G	N
S	J	R
G	N	?

(a) U (b) V
(c) W (d) X

3. The resistance of a 1 km long copper wire of radius 1 mm whose resistivity is 1.72×10^{-8} Ω m is

(a) 5.20 Ω (b) 5.48 Ω
(c) 3.75 Ω (d) 6.50 Ω

4. Find the potential difference across the 20 Ω resistor in the given circuit having a battery of emf 2.5 V.

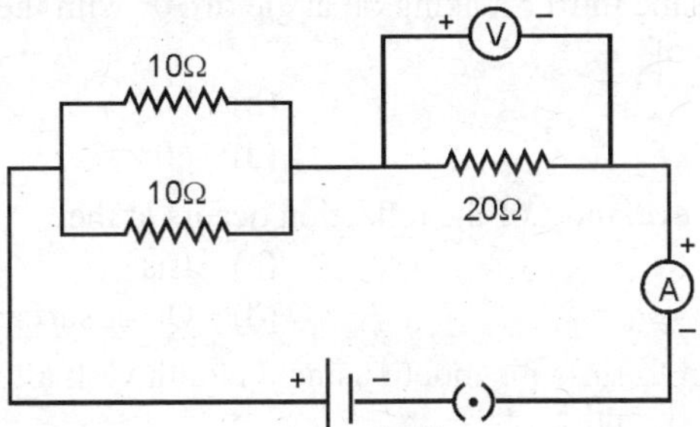

(a) 2 V (b) 3 V
(c) 1 V (d) 5 V

5. The effective resistance between the points A and B in the circuit shown is

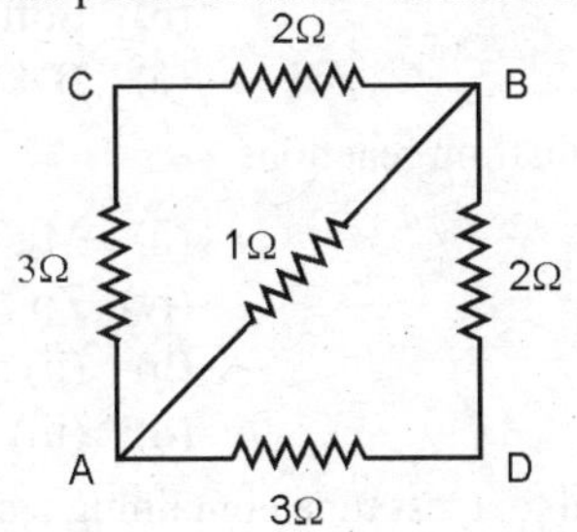

(a) 0.31 Ω (b) 0.51 Ω
(c) 0.71 Ω (d) 0.91 Ω

6. A straight wire of diameter 0.5 mm carrying a current of 1 A is replaced by another wire of 1 mm diameter. The strength of the magnetic field far away is

(a) Twice the earlier value
(b) One half of the earlier
(c) One quarter the earlier value
(d) Same as the earlier value

7. A copper ring having a cut so as not to form a complete loop, is held horizontally and a bar magnet is dropped through the ring with its length along the axis of the ring. The acceleration of the falling magnet is
(a) g
(b) Less than g
(c) More than g
(d) Zero

8. Biogas is a mixture of methane (75%), CO_2 (25%) and traces of
(a) Nitrogen and helium
(b) Helium and hydrogen
(c) Nitrogen and hydrogen
(d) Hydrogen and ethane

9. In a hydro power plant
(a) Potential energy possessed by stored water is converted into electricity
(b) Kinetic energy possessed by stored water is converted into potential energy
(c) Electricity is extracted from water
(d) Water is converted into steam to produce electricity

10. The image formed by a convex mirror of focal length 20 cm is a quarter of the object. What is distance of the object from the mirror ?
(a) + 60 cm
(b) – 60 cm
(c) + 30 cm
(d) – 30 cm

11. A ray of light falls on a plane mirror making on angle of 30° with the mirror. On reflection, the ray deviates through an angle of
(a) 30°
(b) 90°
(c) 120°
(d) 60°

12. When light rays enter the eye, most of the reflection occurs at the
(a) Crystalline lens
(b) Iris
(c) Pupil
(d) Outer surface of the cornea

13. A dentist advises is patient to rinse his mouth using a mouthwash after every meal. What should be the approximate pH of the mouthwash ?
(a) PH= 7
(b) PH > 7
(c) PH = 5.5
(d) None of these

14. Which one of the following will turn red litmus blue ?
(a) Vinegar
(b) Soft drink
(c) Lemon juice
(d) Baking soda solution

15. Which of the following are combination reactions ?
(i) $2\,KClO_3 \xrightarrow{Heat} 2\,KCl + 3O_2$
(ii) $MgO + H_2O \longrightarrow Mg(OH)_2$
(iii) $4\,Al + 3O_2 \longrightarrow 2\,Al_2O_3$
(iv) $Zn + FeSO_4 \longrightarrow ZnSO_4 + Fe$
(a) (i) and (iii)
(b) (ii) and (iii)
(c) (ii) and (iv)
(d) (iii) and (iv)

16. Copper sulphate solution is added to a test tube containing a clean iron nail. The correct description regarding the deposition of copper of the iron nail would be that it starts depositing
(a) At the tip of the nail
(b) In the middle of the nail
(c) Anywhere on the nail
(d) From the head of the nail

17. Mineral acids are stronger acids than carboxylic acids because
(i) Mineral acids are completely ionised

(ii) Carboxylic adids are completely ionised
(iii) Mineral acids are partially ionised
(iv) Carboxylic acids are partially ionised

(a) (ii) and (iii) (b) (i) and (ii)
(c) (i) and (iv) (d) (ii) and (iv)

18. Which one of the following process involve chemical reactions ?
(a) Liquefaction of air
(b) Keeping petrol in a china dish in the open
(c) Storing of oxygen gas under pressure in a gas cylinder
(d) Heating copper wire in presence of air at high temperature

19. Stainless steel is very useful materials a for our life. In stainless steel, iron is mixed with
(a) Ni and Cu (b) Ni and Cr
(c) Cu and Cr (d) Cu and Au

20. Consider the elements given here as a part of the periodic table

a	b	c	d
e	f	g	h
i	j	k	*l*

Choose the correct statements regarding the elements
(i) 'a' is more electropositive than 'd'
(ii) 'h' will form an oxide that is more basic than that formed by 'e'
(iii) The atomic size of the elements increase from 'c' to 'k'

(a) (i) and (ii) (b) (ii) and (iv)
(c) (i) and (iii) (d) None of these

21. What are (i), (ii) and (iii) in the figure ?

(i)	(ii)	(iii)
(a) CH_3COONa	$NaOH$	CH_3COOH
(b) CH_3CH_2COOH	CH_3CH_2OH	$CH_3CH_2COOCH_2CH_3$
(c) $NaOH$	CH_3COOH	CH_3COONa
(d) $CH_3CH_2COOCH_2CH_3$	CH_2CH_2OH	CH_3CH_2COOH

22. Arrange the following elements in the order of their increasing non-metallic character
Li, O, C, Be, F
(a) Li < Be < C < O < F (b) F < O < C Be < Li
(c) F < C < O < Be < Li (d) F < O < Be < C < Li

23. What is the valency of carbon in CH_3-CH_3, $CH_2 = CH_2$ and $CH \equiv CH$?
(a) 2,3,4 (b)2,4,1
(c) only (d) None of the these.

24. Nome the metal used for making the body of aircraft.
(a) Ni (b) Cr
(c) Al (d) Cu

25. What is the chemical name of washing sode?
(a) Sodium carbonte (b) Sodium carbonate monohydrate
(c) Sodium carbonate heptahydrate (d) Sodium carbonate decahydrate

26. which of the following statements regarding holozic nutrition is false?
(a) Holozoic nutrition dores not involve engulfment of whole or part of lant or animal.
(b) Herbiores show holozoic nutrion.
(c) Ingestion, digestion, absorption and assimilation are some of the steps of holozoic nutrition
(d) Cannibals also come under the category of holozoic nutrition.

27. Which of the following increases in muscle cells when they are lacking in oxygen?
(a) Carbon dioxide (b) Lactic acid
(c) Lactose (c) Uric acid

28. Which of the folliwing is most likely to have a much higher breathing rate?
(a) Man (b) Dog
(c) Fish (d) Sparrow.

29. A blood vessel which carries blood back to the heart is :
(a) Artery (b) Vein
(c) Capillary (d) Platelet

30. Darwin's theory of Natural Selection is objected because.
(a) It stresses upon slow and small variations.
(b) It stresses on interspecific competition
(c) It explains that natural calamities take a heavy annual toll of lives.
(d) None of these.

31. The unicellular organism which reproduces by budding is
(a) Spirogyra (b) Hydra
(c) Planaria (d) Yeast

32. One of the following is a surgical method which prevents the sperms from reaching the ovum and pregnancy does not occur. This is method is
(a) Condom (b) Vasectomy
(c) Tubectomy (d) IUCD

33. Which of the following statements are true ?
(i) In males, the Adam's apple is the protruding cartilage of the larynx
(ii) Stomata and lenticels function in gas exchange between the atmosphere and internal tissues.
(iii) While swallowing food, glottis gets covered by small bony flap of skin called epiglottis.
(iv) Reptiles have two chambers in their heart while on the other hand, fish have only one chamber in their heart
(a) (i) and (ii) (b) (ii) and (iii)
(c) (i) and (iii) (d) (ii) and (iv)

34. A trait in an organism is influenced by
(a) Maternal DNA only (b) Paternal DNA only
(c) Both maternal and paternal DNA (d) Neither by paternal nor by maternal DNA

35. Which of the following in an artificial ecosystem ?
(a) Lake (b) Crop field
(c) forest (d) Pond

36. Spore formation is the most common asexual method of reproduction in :
(a) Fungi (b) Algae
(c) Tubers (d) Protozoa

37. The phloem tissue in plants is responsible for the transport of

(a) Water | (b) Sugar
(c) Water and minerals | (d) All of these

38. The question given below has four figures marked 1, 2, 3 and 4 under as problem figures followed by five other figures marked as A, B, C and D and 5 as answer figures. Select one figure from amongst the answer figures which will continue the same series as established by the five problem figures.

Problem Figure

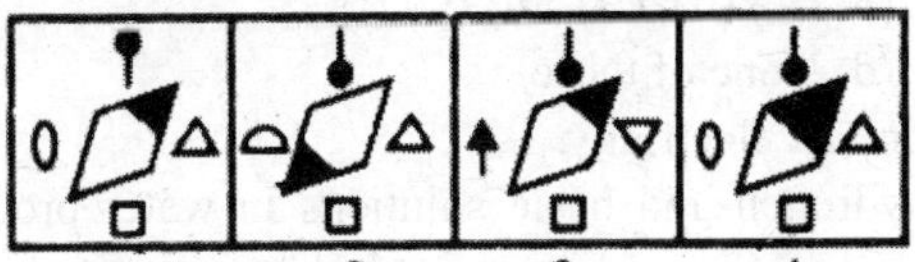

1 2 3 4

Answer Figure

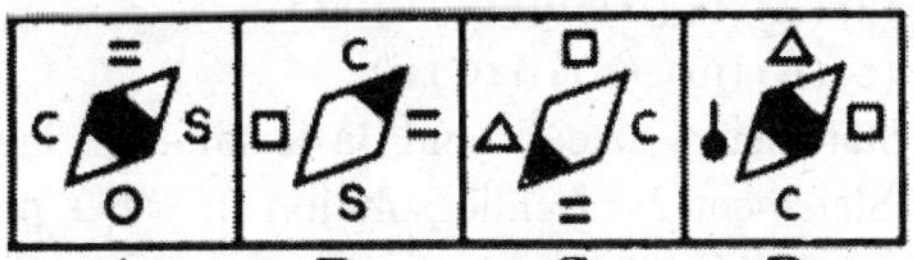

A B C D

39. In the given questions, you are given a combination of alphabets and/or numbers followed by four alternatives (a), (b), (c) and (d). Choose the alternative which most closely resembles the 8 mirror image of the given combination.

C L 9 D G 4 7 2 8

(a) 

(b) 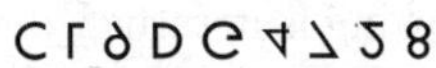

(b) 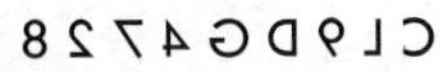

(d) 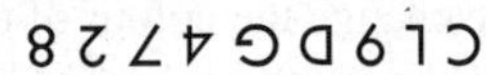

40. In the given question there are three words which have something in common among themselves. Out of four given alternatives choose the most appropriate descriptions about these words:

Tuberculosis : ? :: Myopia : eyes

(a) Ear | (b) Throat
(c) Lungs | (d) Heart

41. In a certain code MONKEY is writes as XDJMNL. How is TIGER written in that code?

(a) QDFHS | (b) SDFHS
(c) SHFDQ | (d) UJHFS

42. Pointing to a servant, a man said, "I have no brother or sister but that man's father is my father's son." Whose servant was it?

(a) His own | (b) His son's
(c) His father's | (d) His nephew's

43. Rajnish walks northwards. After a while, he turns to his right and a little further to his left. Finally, after walking a distances of one Kilometre, he turns to his left again. In which direction is he moving now?

(a) North | (b) South
(c) East | (d) West

44. If A denotes +, B denotes —, C denotes X and D denotes ÷, which of the following statements is correct?

(a) 36C4D8B7A4 = 10 | (b) 16C12A49D7B9 = 200
(c) 32D8C9 = 160B12C12 | (d) 8C8A8D8B = 57

45. .... is a gradual change over a long period, in a form of life.

(a) Evaluation | (b) Evolution
(c) Revolution | (c) Erosion

46. Twinkling of stars is due to atmospheric.

(a) Dispersion of light | (b) Refraction of light
(c) Scattering of light | (d) Internal reflection

47. Charcol is obtained by distinctive distillation of

(a) Wood (b) Coal

(c) Coke (d) Anthracite

48. Match the following:

(A) Ernst Haeckel	(i) Theory of evolutions of the selection
(B) Mendel	(ii) Law of dominance
(C) Darwin	(iii) Father of genetics

(a) (A) (i), (B) (iii) (C) (ii) (b) (A) (ii), (B) (iii) (C) (i)

(c) (A) (iii), (B) (i) (C) ii) (d) None of these

49. Statement 1 : Acidic and Basic solutions in water conduct electricity.

Statement 2 : Acidic solution in water produce hydrogen and basic solutions in water produce hydroxide ions.

(a) Statement 1 is true but statement 2 is false

(b) Statement 2 is true but statement 1 is false

(c) Both statement 1 and statement 2 are true but statement 2 is not a correct reason far statement 1.

(d) Both statement 1 and 2 are true and statement 2 is the correct reason for statement 2.

50. Which of the following is not true?

(a) Lemon juice change the colour of red litmus blue

(b) Bitter gourd change the colour of blue litmus to red

(c) The colour of Methyl orange in the acidic solution is orange

(d) All of these

12 Model Test Paper (NCO)

Mental Ability

1. If in certain code, STUDENT is written as RSTEDMS, then how would TEACHER be written in the same code ?

   (a) SZZDGEQ (b) SZDDGEQ
   (c) SDZDGDQ (d) SDZCGDQ

2. Ramesh started going for regular morning walks for controlling his blood sugar level. He did so for a month and also started taking Yoga lessons, without going for any pathological examination. He underwent pathological test after two months and found that the blood sugar level has come down. Presuming that he had no changed his food habits during these two months, which statement among the alternatives given below follows most logically ?

   (a) Blood sugar level comes down after doing regular morning walk.
   (b) Blood sugar level comes down after doing Yoga.
   (c) Blood sugar level comes down on doing regular morning walk and Yoga
   (d) Regular morning walk, Yoga or both may bring down sugar level despite not changing food habits.

3. Find the number in the position of '?'.

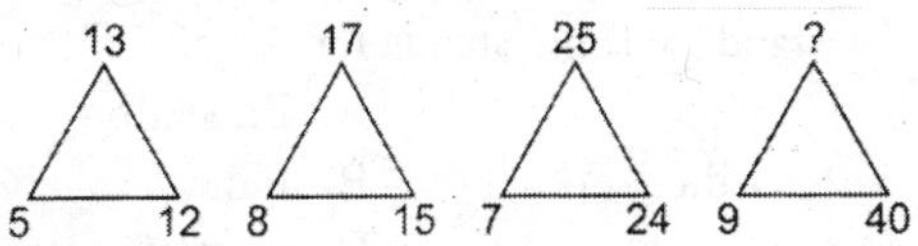

   (a) 41 (b) 45
   (c) 50 (d) 52

4. Identify the number in the position of '?'

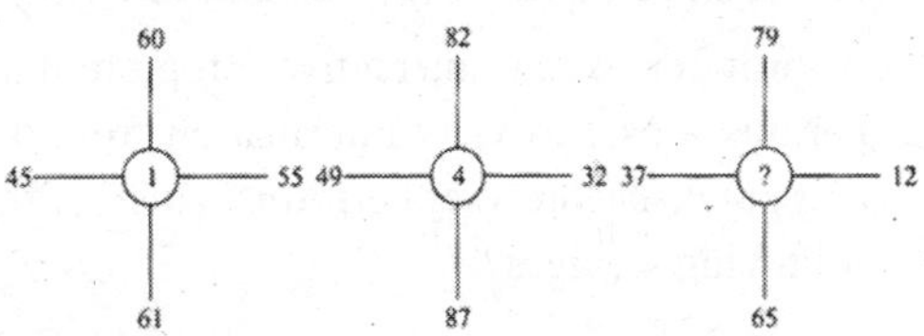

   (a) 2 (b) 3
   (c) 5 (d) 6

5. A sprinter goes off the starting block for 100 m run and at that instant the second-hand of a stopwatch had pointed towards North. He touches the finishing line exactly after 12 seconds. In which direction did the second hand point when he just crossed the finishing line?

   (a) 18° North of East (b) 18° East of North
   (c) 72° North of East (d) 82° East of North

6. Mother was asked how many gifts she had in the bag. She replied that there were all dolls but six, all cars but six, and all books but six. How many gifts had she in all ?

   (a) 9 (b) 18
   (c) 27 (d) 36

7. Question given below has a problem and two statements I & II. Decide if the information given in the statement is sufficient for answering the problem: K, R, S and T are four players in Indian Cricket team. Who is the oldest among them?

   I. The total age of K & T together is more than that of S
   II. The total age of R & K together is less than that of S.

   (a) Data in statement I alone is sufficient
   (b) Data in statement II alone is sufficient
   (c) Data in both statements together is sufficient
   (d) Data in both statement together is not sufficient

8. In a diary, there are 60 cows and buffalos. The number of cows is twice that of buffalos. Buffalo X ranked seventeenth in terms of milk delivered. If there are 9 cows ahead of

Buffalo. X, how many buffalos are after in rank in terms of milk delivered ?

(a) 10 (b) 11
(c) 12 (d) 13

Logical & Analytical Reasoning

9. In a group of persons working in a software company, 6 persons can operate on DOS, 15 can operate onwindows operating system and 6 can operate on Linux. In that group none can operate on any other operating system. If 2 persons in the group can work on two operating systems and one person canwork on all the three, then how many persons are there in the group?
(a) 21 (b) 22
(c) 23 (d) 24

10. Four persons Alok, Bhupesh, Chandu and Dinesh have a total of Rs. 100 among themselves. Alok andBhupesh between them have as much money as Chandu and Dinesh between them but Alok has moremoney than Bhupesh, and Chandu has only half the money that Dinesh has. Alok has in fact Rs. 5 morethan Dinesh. Who has the most money?
(a) Alok (b) Bhupesh
(c) Chandu (d) Dinesh

11. The letters L, M, N, O, P, Q, R, S and T in their order are substituted by nine integers 1 to 9 but not in thatorder. 4 is assigned to P. The difference between P and T is 5. The difference between N and T is 3.What is the integer assigned to N ?
(a) 7 (b) 5
(c) 4 (d) 6

12. Six roads lead to a country. They may be indicated by letters X, Y, Z and digits 1, 2, 3. When there is storm, Yis blocked. When there are floods X, 1 and 2 will be affected. When road 1 is blocked, Z also is blocked. At atime when there are floods and a storm also blows, which road(s) can be used ?
(a) Z and 2 (b) Only Z
(c) Only 3 (d) Only Y

13. Two important characteristics of a hypothesis are that it should be testable and that it should be stated ina manner that it can be refuted. Which one of the following hypothesis, fulfills these characteristics?
(a) Intelligent persons have good memory
(b) Some birds are animals
(c) Some businessmen are dishonest
(d) All men are mortal

Computers & Information Technology

14. What is the addition of 101010 with 111111?
(a) 1101001 (b) 1001001
(c) 1111001 (d) 1100001

15. Modern Computers do not work with decimal numbers. Instead they process binary numbers, groupsof 0's and 1's because
(a) Electronic devices are most reliable when designed for two state (binary) operation
(b) Binary circuits are simple
(c) Memory is only possible for binary numbers
(d) With decimal numbers, the circuits are complex and costly

16. Debug is a term denoting
(a) Error correction processs
(b) Writing of instructions in developing a new program
(c) Fault detection in equipment
(d) Determining useful life

17. Match the following terms with what they stand forTerm Stands for

1. .Com	A. Education
2. .Edu	B. India
3. .In	C. Australia
4. .Au	D. Commerce

(a) 1A, 2B, 3C, 4D (b) 1B, 2C, 3D, 4A
(c) 1C, 2D, 3A, 4B (d) 1D, 2A, 3B, 4C.

18. A browser is an interactive program that permits a user to view information from the computer. Thebrowser performs which of the following services?

(a) Connecting to the source computer whose address is specified
(b) Requesting new page from the source
(c) Receiving new page
(d) All of these.

19. Modern Computers compared to earlier computers are
(a) Faster and larger
(b) Less reliable
(c) Larger and stronger
(d) Faster and smaller.

20. Who is regarded as the Father of computers?
(a) Abacus
(b) John Napier
(c) Pascal
(d) Charles Babbage

Cyber Olympiad

- Introduction to Computer
- Fundamentals of Computer
- Parts of Computer
- Uses of Computer
- Learning to Use Keyboard
- Learning to Use Mouse
- Introduction to MS Paint ✶ Latest Developments in IT ✶ Patterns
- Odd One Out
- Series Completion
- Analogy
- Coding and Decoding
- Ranking Test
- Embedded Figures
- Grouping of Figures
- Measuring Units
- Geometrical Shapes
- High Order Thinking Skills
- Short Answer Questions
- Model Test Paper

- Fundamentals of Computer
- Generations of Computer
- MS Paint
- MS Word 2010
- Introduction to Internet
- Latest Development in IT
- Patterns
- Odd One Out
- Series Completion
- Analogy and Classification
- Coding and Decoding
- Ranking and Alphabet Test
- Mirror and Water Images
- Days, Dates and Time
- Geometrical Shapes
- High Order Thinking Skills
- Short Answer Questions
- Model Test Paper

- Fundamentals of Computer
- Evolution of Computer
- MS Word 2010
- MS Paint ✶ Network
- Internet and Its Uses ✶ Windows 7
- Latest Developments in IT ✶ Patterns
- Analogy and Classification
- Coding and Decoding
- Alphabet and Ranking Test
- Direction Sense Test ✶ Mirror and Water Images
- Geometrical Shapes and Solids
- Time and Calendar
- High Order Thinking Skills
- Short Answer Questions
- Model Test Paper

- Fundamentals of Computer
- Memory and Storage Devices
- Introduction to Multimedia
- MS Paint ✶ MS Word 2010 ✶ MS PowerPoint 2010
- Windows 7
- Network
- Internet
- Latest Development in IT
- Patterns ✶ Analogy and Classification
- Coding and Decoding
- Ranking and Alphabet Test
- Direction Sense Test ✶ Mirror and Water Images
- Geometrical Shapes and Angles ✶ High Order Thinking Skills ✶ Short Answer Questions
- Model Test Paper

visit our online bookstore: **www.vspublishers.com**